HUES OF MY LIFE

SHRADDHA RAI

Contents

Contents

Preface

'HUES OF MY LIFE' is a book basically based on the different types of emotions experienced by a person during the journey of life. Anxiety, contentment, depression, envy, fear, anger, pride are the shades of one's personality which are revealed during different time intervals. This book is a collection of these emotions wrapped into poetry.

In addition, it also contains some poems written on some special festivals & important personalities which bring the glimpses of history & magic of motivation.

The author tried to cover all the topics suggested by her heart & presented them with pure thoughts, alluring words & relatable verses.

Preface

H[illegible] is a book basically based on the different types of emotions experienced by a person during the journey of life. And it contains [illegible] happiness, envy, fear, anger, pride [illegible] and so on. [illegible] personality [illegible] during different [illegible]. This book is a [illegible] of these emotions wrapped [illegible].

In addition, it also contains some poems [illegible] some special [illegible] & [illegible] personalities which bring [illegible] of history & [illegible] of motivation.

The author tried to cover all the [illegible] [illegible] pieces [illegible] pure thoughts [illegible].

About Author

Shraddha Rai

She is a young poetess hailing from the City of Lakes, Bhopal, Madhya Pradesh. She is a student studying in fourth year & pursuing B.Sc-B.Ed. Her hobby is writing, gardening & playing. She loves to paint the canvas of her life with the vibrant colors of thoughts, emotions & experiences. She has written 100+ anthologies as a co-author. In addition, she compiled an anthology named 'GARDEN OF LIFE'. Furthermore, she has written a solo book named 'INK FROM A KIND HEART' in the year 2021 which is available on Amazon. She shares her write-ups through social media platforms like Instagram s_ilent_killer27 and on YourQuote & Oxigle as Shraddha Rai. You can follow her to read her write-ups.

Acknowledgements

I would like to express a deep sense of thanks & gratitude to the co-founder & CEO of WOS publication for guiding me immensely throughout the course of my project. They always evinced keen interest in my work. Their constructive advice & constant motivation has been responsible for the successful completion of my anthology.

My sincere thanks goes to Ms. Nikita Dudagi, founder of Words of soul publication for her coordination in extending every possible support for the completion of this book. I am also thankful to my parents for their support. Last but not the least, I would like to thank God for giving me strength, wisdom & grace to make my creative ideas & thoughts into mesmerizing words.

We all are happy & excited giving you this book filled with different emotions experienced by an individual during their life span. I hope you will find a great & worthy content in this book.

Happy Reading!!

Disclaimer

We are publishing this book under Words of soul publication.
We have tried our best to make this book free from plagiarism in the write-ups of the author and her work featured in this book.
Our editors tried their best to make the content enchanting and free from errors & spelling mistakes.

1. Words of soul

In the depth of ocean & beside those tiny shells,
My heart is crawling over the humid dust of surface.
Yearning to imbibe the drops of shaded & pure smiles,
To engross an indispensable luminance within myself.
My soul is uttering notes to touch every region of this ocean,
To reach the realms & perspectives of bloomin' pearls.
And my mind is aspiring to craft new enchanting fables,
Into my envisioned world free from the black holes of negativity.
My inner self is ready to rely on the divine grace of Lord,
Which embellishes every part of me with positive flowers.

2. Years

Years gone still a soul is living in the castle of my heart,
His mellifluous voice always resides in every corner of my mind.
I can feel the sound of his name through my running heartbeat,
The enchanting vibes of our special moments are still flowing in my veins.
Years to decades are running one after the other in full speed,
But, your last rose is not ready to lose its fragrance.
Our pics are still blooming with the vibes of our love,
Your gifts are still reflecting your romantic mood.
The evenings with the colorful sky still holding you with the shining stars,
The nature also tries to create your facial expressions every night.
You are really a lucky man with thousands of lovers,
Who constantly try to create you in their own enchanting ways.

3. Bud of mercy

A unique bud which needs to be bloomed in everyone's heart,
Take people think above their own business charts.
It is something which adds a shade in the sky of humanity,
And work as an essence in the decorated cake of one's personality.
Feeling the pain of others & applying the ointment of kindness in their wounds,
Removes the thorns & stones of your life without any pounds.
Mercy itself is a precious worship of God without any doubt,
Which purifies the heart & soul from inside out.

4. Three delightful souls

Over the skies, across my imaginative streets of landscape,
I found three eminent souls with utmost innocence.
From dusk until dawn we loved to omit numerous crafty jokes,
Not even a second allowed to pass without witnessing our realms.
Walking together in the meadow of life to dive in the majestic pages of future,
Drifted from the chaos to glint in the moonlit above the horizon.
Sprinkle rejoicing vibes in the stardust of innumerable plights,
Excluding scars of each other, we loved to do breathtaking adventures.
We may not be consanguineous by habits but, we're the apt description of euphoria,
Who loved to bumfuzzle people through abundant ways to deal with troubles.
Fate pushed us to penetrate in our diary of memories,
To glorify every page with some enthralling tales.

5. Unexpressed emotions

An entrancing eve full of contentment & notes of music,
I was enjoying & capturing moments in my camera.
Suddenly, I saw a new face with an unbeatable glow,
I was lost in the hues coming out from that pious soul.
Time stopped & my heart pushed me towards a new journey,
I was moving towards him with a bundle of unexpressed emotions.
My heart started portraying my emotions on a blank paper,
Which gonna reveal a blueprint of the vibes of my new destination.

6. Toxic talks of 2 AM

Light off & conversations on in the atmosphere of silence,
Emotions are flooding from the heart with no barriers.
Fingers are busy in conveying the hidden thoughts through messages,
Words are flowing like a breeze hitting each other's heart.
From sharing the moments without the adulteration of toxic desires,
Now you're firing the words after dipping in the venom of virulent intentions.
I owe you for being my healer, now I prefer not to stay in the prison of your dark thoughts,
Your advices were the ointment to my wounds, presently working as a toxin.
It was my fault for being addicted to the soft layer of your personality,
From sending n number of messages & exchanging emotions.
Currently I want to be a statue having sealed lips & tied hands,
Who is powerful enough to grow with the thorns & flowers of its emotions.

7. Moonlight walk with my love

A beautiful night full of moonlight which is free from all the layers of darkness,
I am walking & talking to my love about the shades of our love story.
The moon is smiling & ready to spray thousands of blessings for us,
Trees around us are witnessing our lovely conversations with blushing expressions.
The cold breeze is blowing so fast & tries to push me towards you,
The euphonious sound of swaying waves are encouraging me to convey my love.
I feel like the nature is ready to project a reel of the jubilant moments of our love,
Today I wanna paint this whole sky with the bright colors of our love.
I wanna eradicate all the factors spoiling our precious moments,
Just wish to spend the entire night with you & our well-wisher 'moon'.
Hey, my love, are you ready to walk with me until the moon?
Where we can create our dream castle which will become a reflection of our love.
Be my everlasting companion & trust me this journey has numerous ecstatic surprises,
I just want everyone to taste the flavor of love & fill this world with the magic of love.

8. Story of a burning soul

I'm drowning in the black sea of depression without a pinch of hope,
My eyes are eagerly waiting to see the sun of positive vibes.
Above the brown mountains, my soul lost somewhere in the stardust,
Thoughts are slipping from all the corners of my mind.
The astonishing fragrance of my soul is mixing with the impure vibes,
The worms of negativity are dancing all over my body.
Which is burning my soul with the spicy essence of emotions,
Now, I got a new healer in the form of wave of love.
Which have the power to wash all the worries & pains,
And blessed me with the potential to achieve the impossible.

9. Glance of windy days

Occupied by thousand tasks in a day,
My souls is orienting itself towards a new window of hope.
To inhale the blithesome vibes of this era,
I'm vibing alone in the activated mode of new versions.
Erasing the names of my dear ones from my compassionate heart,
To encourage my soul to breathe freely.
Clearing all the segments of trash stored in my mind,
To embrace myself with gracious sparkles of almighty.
Enjoying in the journey of unseen adventures,
& experienced that your flaws makes you flawless.

10. Air of melancholy

Under the cloudy sky & over the humid dust,
I'm vibing alone with a heavy heart in the air of melancholy.
Entering a world of insecurity & sadness,
Hoping to move out soon from this alienated phase.
My soul is thirsty for some satisfying drops,
To create blissful moments every way,
Once I'll move out from this chaos,
I'll never look back & invest myself for others.

11. A journey filled with emotions

Slowly & steadily, I'm moving closer to my sunshine,
After crossing the dark shadows of my path.
My soul is filling itself with the sweet nectar of your thoughts,
And my heart is craving for a single glance of your face.
I'm ready to face a thousand hurdles to breathe in your aroma,
Your place has a sparkling aura enlightening every cell of my body.
These deserted paths witnessed you so many times,
Now narrating your alluring fables in front of me.
This journey is normal yet magical for me,
As every region has hundreds of stored glimpses of you.
I'm coming…
Not to meet you, but to feel you.

12. Levitating

Glorifying the pages of life with profound colors,
My zealous soul is levitating above the mountains of conflict.
Erupting the drops of positivity in every region,
It is dancing joyfully across all streets of landscape.

13. Pain of a smiling picture

Amidst the chaos & vulnerabilities of life,
Some pearls are searching new ways to survive.
With a bud of hope in their compact hearts,
Snaps are smiling with hidden pain in ravishing arts.
Engulfing all the flames of melancholy,
Little birds are attempting to add moments of jolly.
Let's endeavor to craft a new rainbow of inspiring hues,
Which will help to utter magical words with dazzling views.

14. It's ok not to be ok

When no one is there to pull you towards the zone of positivity,
Be your master to rely on the caboodle of good thoughts.
Don't abandon yourself while searching for close ones,
Feeling alienated sometimes help you to grow in right direction.

15. A magical journey

Our college is the living witness of your adorable activities,
The walls still project your cute yet naughty expressions.
Gates of every classroom glancing for your single glimpse,
The atmosphere is full of the mellifluous echoes of your name.
Stairs still preserving the imprints of your footsteps,
Benches awaiting to see you sitting & studying.
The paths yearning to hear your footsteps,
Come back!! This world is waiting for your presence.

16. Sin and sinners

Shedding the dark leaves of yesterday from the evergreen present,
Loving myself is becoming a sin for the unwanted weeds.
Steadily, my soul is distancing myself from the so-called society of intelligence,
Looking for eternal peace in the crowd of this modern era.
My happiness is ready to rely on tiny butterflies of success,
This ultimate aroma of amusement lies in all areas of my mind.
Surviving in this world of sinners with a flame of purity,
Is taking my soul to a beguiling zone of almighty.

17. Colors of life

The diary of my life is a plethora of nostalgic moments,
Ready to whisper soulful words of positivity & amusements.
Fate is pushing me to walk over the clouds of heaven,
To inhale the vibes of serenity which adds a new impression.

18. Jumping for joy

Hey love, do you remember that foggy evening of Sunday?
When I was going to reveal the feelings of my heart.
My cheeks were red & my eyes were smiling with love,
My heart was jumping for joy & awaiting to see your reaction.
The undulating waves of love were hitting my soul & shouting your name,
I felt the vibrations of the mesmerizing songs which came from the corners of my mind.
The magical words were moving in every part of my body like the magnetic impulses,
And activated all areas by sprinkling the powder of love.
The balloons of smileys were flying around me in infinite number,
That day was really a wonderful one in bringing the unlimited packets of happiness.
For some point of time I was stuck in the border of reality & imagination,
Then I realized that I was dancing in the real world under the rainfall of love.
I was trapped in the web of joy & I wished to live there forever with my love,
Until my last breath I wanna stay with you without a single break.
After death we'll shine in the sky of love in the form of stars,
And will encourage people to add the shade of love in their life's sketchbook like us.

19. Winter : Season of love

O winter, I was waiting for you since so long,
Finally you arrived with the waves of cold breeze.
In the heart-warming fragrance of roses & daffodils,
I wanna add another magical aroma of love.
In the foggy morning of Sunday, I saw you standing near bus stop,
Me in your favorite black hoodie wants you to notice me.
Suddenly, a thousand-carat smile strikes on my face,
Which bring splendid shades from my radiant soul.
I lost my mind in the luminance of your glorious persona,
Whereas my heart is waiting to collab with your flawless soul.

20. Do you still miss me?

Do you still miss me?
Or is it just me who is living in the enchanting world of our precious memories?
Do you still remember our late night conversations?
Or is it just me who read our old chats every day?
Do you still care about me?
Or is it just me who is worried for you every second?
Do you still feel that I am more than your bestie?
Or is it just me who remember the glimpses of our bond?
Do you still have my picture in your heart?
Or is it just me who feel you every night by listening to my heartbeat?
Do you still feel attached to me?
Or is it just me who tries every possible way to connect you?
Do you still feel the same as before?
Or is it just me who is feeling all these?
Do I still come in your dreams?
Or is it just me who is dreaming about you?
Do you still have that wish of going out for a long drive with me?
Or is it just me who is eagerly waiting for that beautiful day?
Do you still miss me?
Or is it just me who is missing you every moment?

21. Power of three magical words

Those magical words you whispered in my ears with the fragrance of love,
Brings a unique current of the vibes of your love in my nerves.
The flavor of your love is slowly mixing with the simplicity & purity of my soul,
And adds an alluring essence to my emotionless personality.
My heart beat is running like a bullet train for some moments,
The atmosphere surrounded me is filled with the echo of those magical words.
My eyes started shining with gleaming shade due to the magic of love,
I'm flying high with the wings of love in the blue sky of my imagination.
Today I realized the power of those magical words which brings a new version of mine,
My lips sealed & my ears are eagerly waiting to hear those words again.
My eyes don't have any wish to open again & see the reality,
I just wanna lost in my imaginary world of love having open gate for lovers.
The magic of those words still have an impact on my mind & heart,
My body doesn't want to move anywhere to create a hindrance in the magical journey.
I want to move bit by bit, experiencing the love vibes in the way to our dream castle,
I wish this journey should end with lots of soothing & joyful moments.

22. Humanity

A precious emotion lives in the heart of every human,
Which reveals God's blessings & love in a great fusion.
Love & kindness for others are its versions,
Which can vary from person to person.
Does humanity still alive?
Do people still help others to survive?
Decades one after the other,
We are losing humanity due to race & color.
People are judged by status & religion,
Which develops a layer of dark dust in our vision.
Ignoring other's sufferings & pains,
Just for our benefits & gains.
Let's try to bring the real image of humans,
Which is God gifted apart from any illusions.
Let's join hands for the development of humanity,
Which will make you a great personality.

23. Crushed soul

With hundreds of dreams decorated in my eyes,
You came with a fake smile with thousands of lies.
I closed my eyes & wanted to dive in the colourful pages,
But you trapped my soft soul in millions of unwanted cages.
I never forget that moment when you kicked my feelings,
Which crushed my soul & closed all doors of healings.

24. Enjoying under the stars

We are staying so far,
Still enjoying under the stars.
Sitting on the roof of the house,
We are collecting memories which were our powerhouse.
Let's go in the lap of stars,
Coz the people constantly try to burn your dreams like a cigar.
This greedy world of fakeness & trends,
Where no one is there to hold your hands.
Don't let your desires sink,
Take a stand for you and think.

25. Happiness

On the morning of my b'day sunlight was crawling under my bed,
Me with sleepy eyes awaited to hold the gleaming rays.
All the surrounding creatures turned blue & red,
Gifted me a decorated tiara of flowers to splash vibes until a thousand days.

26. Darkness

It is darkness all around me full of magical thoughts,
Pulling my soft soul in front of tough roads.
My hands are yearning to pen down unseen poems,
Which are helping me in sprouting the new seeds of creativity.

27. Love

Love is a beautiful feeling & an ultimate way to find solace,
With the involvement of million hearts & God's grace.
People seems busy in pretending their efforts for a bright future,
Amidst the situations, love has power to melt hard sculpture.
There may be a thousand ways to reveal love for a person,
But unconditional & selfless care always be the prime one.
The aura of love is full of the lullabies of nostalgic moments,
When the pretty faces smile without being the beauty pageants.
Love is an update for the selfish outdated souls,
To reach out into a new version of positivity in different roles.
Which enable the destruction of the bugs of envy & hatred,
And fix the buds of love & peace from getting degraded.

28. 12 months of 2021

Tender pages of 2021 are turning slowly & slowly,
With some unexpected chapters having unseen stories.
Hey January!! Do you remember our fearful memories of exam days?
Dear February, you were truly wonderful in creating a frame for lovebirds.
Umm… March!! I couldn't forget your amazing days of bunk & movies,
And April!! How can I forget your stressful & boring days?
Dear May!! You were so long & hot as always with the vibes of laziness,
Aah June!! I'm so grateful for your soothing & alluring moments.
Here comes my favorite month… Guessing?
Ya it's July!! Which brings ecstatic surprises for me every year on my birthday.
Hola August!! I still remember your nonstop holidays of festivals & fun,
Emm September… it's your turn, you were a bunch of unforgettable meetings.
Now comes October, which came with a new journey of enthralling twists & turns,
Yup!! Dear November… I really enjoyed your days which were a great combo of anxiety & pleasure.
O December!! Being a mystery you're passing slowly, but remember you have to reveal it soon.
This is the overview of some chapters of 2021.

29. Glimpse of a charming soul

A lovely girl decorated with the sparkles of dreams,
Who eliminates the barriers of her passion of unique themes.
She discloses her new areas of interest,
Which embraces her persona with love & trust.
Hey sweetie!! Do you still remember our unplanned hangouts?
Which were the reasons of our shimmering faces.
I'm still smiling remembering the nights full of doubts,
When we were contestants of our career races.
Staying in this shatterproof bond of friendship,
I owe you for bringing profound moments of joy.
On your special day, I'm adding new pearls of love to our relationship,
Which will rejuvenate ourselves with a million moments to enjoy.

30. Searching myself beyond clouds

Stuck in this world of fakeness & trends,
There I lost myself from every end.
I found dark clouds during my journey,
Raindrops are coming from them like money.
I feel like these clouds entered my heart & raining heavily,
& fills the water with pain inside my soul slowly.
Now it makes me feel disheartened,
As my mind & heart is completely darkened.
My search is still on to find my real soul,
& this is my last and ultimate goal.

31. 7 colors of rainbow

Just like the shades of your personality,
Which reveals your originality.
Red signifies your anger,
Which couldn't stay so longer.
Yellow signifies your fruity behavior,
Which never lets you face any failure.
Blue signifies your peaceful nature,
Which makes you a unique creature.
Green signifies your broad thinking,
Which helps you to sharp you writing.
Violet signifies your depressed mood,
Which can be change by healthy food.
Orange signifies the purity of your soul,
Which gives you courage & dedication to reach your goal.
Indigo signifies a dark side which makes you a devil,
& that's your ultimate power to fight with any evil.

32. Dreams

A small word with thousands of hopes,
Helps a soul to reach above the slopes.
It sprinkles millions of positive vibes,
Which opens countless ways to shine from unseen sides.
Dreams are something which needs efforts & dedication,
To achieve the targets with a strong determination.
Dreams makes a person passionate towards goals,
& helps to stand confidently like strong poles.
Dreams add a gleaming shade to our eyes,
Coz it's a precious gift which brings numerous smiles.
It's truly a soothing moment which remove all the fears,
& helps us to shine in every age with hidden tears.

33. Caged bird

Living in a society with narrow-minded people who're ready with a long list of restrictions,
I am searching the open sky to fly with the wings of my dreams.
People are always ready to spread the dust of negativity in front of my steps,
Still I feel God's hand on my head which release the positive vibes inside my mind.
Every night I'm trying to protect myself from the blanket of negativity
Because it brings a giant tornado of harmful & depressing thoughts.
I am living happily with my well-wishers but still, I feel like a caged bird,
Who is under the cage of outdated mentalities & boundaries.
They constantly try to ruin my eternal peace with their unwanted bullets of jealousy & arrogance,
Smiling outside & burning inside due to my success can be observed by their behavior.
The thorns & stones which are thrown by my haters motivates me to walk with extra care,
I won't stop until I find a way to create my own galaxy with zero percent darkness.
I am collecting bundles of positivity inside my soul to break this cage,
Which helps me to inject the positive vibes in the minds of people.
It will stop them from sowing the seeds of hatred & jealousy;
It will protect their upcoming generation from the harmful weeds of negativity.

34. India : A precious paradise

A beautiful garden having numerous unique flowers as religions,
Who attract different butterflies with the help of culture & traditions.
These butterflies love to stay in particular flower of their choice,
Flowers as states helps them to succeed & raise their voice.
They suck the nectar of languages from the flowers helps them to grow,
& encourages their development & smooth flow.
These flowers bloom happily with the help of nutrients of ancient knowledge coming from the soil,
This soil like India is the mother of all flowers who prevents them to spoil.
This is the pride & specialty of India,
Where we get the precious knowledge on things as encyclopedia.
This is truly an alluring paradise,
Where all forms of God are worshiped & people have the right to choose & advise.
India is also blessed with the astounding biodiversity,
Which have unique organisms & variety.
India is the heart of every Indian
Because it is a precious paradise for every citizen.

35. Love for a heavenly soul

My mind is roaming in the corners of the world,
Just to collect the shattered pieces of my soul.
Like a solitary boat lost in the middle of ocean,
My heart is willingly searching your presence.
Scribbling words displaying the clips of my past,
Compelling me to love you more & more every second.
I didn't spend much moments with you, still your departure broken me,
Often the scent of despondence surrounds me completely.
I couldn't rely thoroughly on my frail heart,
As it is lamenting every sphere of my life.
You're alive in the dwellings of our heart,
And smiling alluringly eliminating all the sorrows.

36. B.R. Ambedkar : A man of virtues

Gone are the days embraced by the efforts of an inspiring personality,
Who used to work selflessly for every section of society.
Entwined by innumerable obstacles in the path of success,
He worked every hour to eliminate every shadow of distress.
Being a real devotee of India, pushed him to bring the supreme law,
'The Constitution of India', to frame the principles of every row.
His imperishable rope of thoughts is truly a bunch of motivation,
Release positive vibes in every sphere of life to encourage amplification.

37. Emotions for a pious soul

My soul is levitating around the clouds of heaven,
To see & feel your presence again.
Drifted by the waves of time, my heart still yearning for you,
The pages of past still have an imprint on my present.
Our snaps are still shimmering with the aroma of your personality,
Dark days arrived, firing the bullets of utmost sadness.
Still I feel the euphonious rhythm of your lullabies,
My messy hairs still remember your gentle touch.
I can feel you every moment in numerous ways,
You're alive within myself as a prestigious pearl.

38. Voice of selenophile

Dear moon, your spectacular yet soothing smile made me to fall for you every way,
Shadows lurking behind you're drenched by your pious essence every day.
My heart craves to gleam like you with the aroma of my realms,
You're merely a creation of nature but for me, a basket of prestigious gems.

39. Constellations : A magical world

A magical world which looks so beautiful,
Helps to spread the fragrance of memories to make the night meaningful.
It helps to convey our inner thoughts to our beloved ones,
By shooting those lovely words through virtual guns.
Countless stars appear to form a unique pattern,
Which help people to orient themselves with a turn.
Hydra, Virgo, Hercules, Cetus & Ursa Major,
Shows the alluring & elegant forms of nature.
It offers a special feel in the heart,
Coz it hits our mind like a dart.
This world sprinkles thousands of positive vibes,
Which speaks our hidden feelings from unseen sides.
It's a precious gift which brings numerous smiles,
& adds a gleaming shade to our eyes.
It's truly a soothing moment which remove all the fears,
& helps us to smile in every age with hidden tears.

40. Vibes of my world

41. Nature : An astounding paradise

A place where millions of creatures surviving together,
Glistening in their ways with the support of each other.
From dawn until dusk, they visit numerous regions of landscapes,
Sparkling rays of moon decorate them with contentment leaving no gaps.
Imbibing the drops of water from the natural sources quench their thirst,
Tiny insects dancing peacefully in all trees above the humid dust.
Mountains are smiling in mystical ways despite the hurdles,
Rivers are glancing seamlessly with the merry bundles.
Flowers started furnishing the atmosphere with their dazzling fragrance,
Butterflies are ready to add more hues to illuminate every sense.
Waves are penetrating into the sand castles of shore,
Blowing breeze offering hidden scenes hitting the heart's core.
Nature is nourishing its creatures today by its divine vibes,
To embrace every segment of the globe & growing lives.

42. Happy Holi

Drenched in the vibrant colors & shades of love,
People are dancing on Holi tunes all over the globe.
Having sweets in one hand & gulal in the other,
Faces occupied with numerous hues together.
Wishing you all a very Happy Holi from the core of my heart,
Keep working on yourself to step forward for a powerful start.
Have faith in almighty who blessed you with the right guidance,
Stay positive & keep working hard to create a difference.

43. Aura of Christmas

Cakes, gifts, Christmas trees & vibes of carols,
Little ones waiting for the arrival of Santa Claus.
Unique & heart-warming decorations in churches,
Christmas Eve come with the melodies of delicate lips.
Across the white snow, tall maples & conifers,
Hundreds of ears are thirsty to hear the bells of reindeer.
It's a glorious eve which brings the imprint of Christ in our heart,
And minimizes all the hidden trash from our souls.
Celebration ends with the index of the upcoming year,
Having fresh promises, hopes & desires featuring ourselves.

44. Republic Day

Millions of patriots lost their lives just for the sake of humanity,
Where the detractors were busy in establishing new kingdoms.
After fighting for decades, finally we got a chance to rise & shine,
In this era of complete freedom, we're free to explore the areas of our choice.
'Republic Day' is the memorial of our brave martyrs,
Who had done countless efforts for the development of constitution.
This supreme law featured the transition of the country to a republic,
Every year a grand celebration conducted with the notes of patriotic songs & parades.
To decorate this pious day with the vibes & sparkles of history,
And to renew our energies for witnessing new victories in the future.

45. Journey with WOS

An outstanding journey with numerous twists & turns,
Which boosts my soul with great dedication & confidence.
WOS is a wonderful ocean with astounding & unique pearls,
Who shines in their creative ways by spraying their alluring words.
Every day a new challenge is given which helps to reflect the magic of our style,
And brings a tone of motivation through the unexpected surprises.
The admins are really unbeatable in giving the opportunities to the newbies,
Which provides the way to spray the vibes of their talent & skills.
I love to write for the challenges & inhaling new words & ideas,
Now WOS reached 1 year after loads of hard work & hurdles.
My wishes & blessings are always with you without any full stop,
May your community reach until sky with great talents & personalities.
(This poetry is dedicated to WOS community)

46. Guru : A motivational soul

A Guru has to play a lot of roles,
To motivate their students towards their goals.
Guru can convert a broken mirror like student,
Into a shining diamond with a tone of improvement.
Relationship of Guru & Shishya is very precious,
Helps a student to learn & become ambitious.
Guru Purnima is a special day dedicated to spiritual & academic gurus,
Who made us a good human with their discipline & rules.
They are enlightened humans who are ready to share their knowledge,
From a small school to a big college.
They don't expect anything in return,
Just want students to understand the things & learn.

Thank You Note

Thanks a tone for your valuable time to read my book patiently. Will bring next book soon with new thoughts, astounding experiences & dazzling verses.

'Be a positive thinker who is ready to spread the aroma of its thoughts.'

Shraddha Rai

(Author)

Printed by Libri Plureos GmbH in Hamburg,
Germany